NEW MATH CHESS

NEW MATH CHESS

Educational and Recreational
Two-Player Game

Promoting

Numerical Skill, Speedy Calculation, Strategic Thinking,
Memory Improvement, Concentration, Decision-Making,
Perseverance, Logic, Observation, Problem Solving,
Analysis, and Organization Skill

Dr George Ho

Copyright © 2020 by Dr George Ho.

Library of Congress Control Number: 2020912926
ISBN: Hardcover 978-1-9845-0690-0
Softcover 978-1-9845-0689-4
eBook 978-1-9845-0691-7

All rights reserved. No part of this book may be reproduced or transmitted in any form or by any means, electronic or mechanical, including photocopying, recording, or by any information storage and retrieval system, without permission in writing from the copyright owner.

Any people depicted in stock imagery provided by Getty Images are models, and such images are being used for illustrative purposes only.
Certain stock imagery © Getty Images.

Print information available on the last page.

Rev. date: 07/29/2020

To order additional copies of this book, contact:
Xlibris
AU TFN: 1 800 844 927 (Toll Free inside Australia)
AU Local: 0283 108 187 (+61 2 8310 8187 from outside Australia)
www.Xlibris.com.au
Orders@Xlibris.com.au
814352

To my wife, C.T.N. Minh, for her support, patience, and inspiration.

To my children, H.T.M. Tâm, H.H. Hiệp, H.H. Trí, H.T.M. Châu.

In memory of my beloved parents, H.V. Giá, T.T. Tòng.

H.V. Hoà

PREFACE OF NEW MATH CHESS

New Math Chess is a new edition of *Mathematical Chess* published in 2018.

Mathematical Chess is a two-player educational and recreational game played on ten Digit pieces (0, 1, 2, 3, 4, 5, 6, 7, 8, 9) and six Operator pieces (Addition, Subtraction, Multiplication, Division, Power (Square & Cube), and Root (Square Root & Cube Root)). The Chessboard is a grid made up of nine vertical and nine horizontal lines.

A chess piece can move freely on any horizontal or vertical line provided other chess pieces do not obstruct it. A move of a chess piece can result in the removal of the opponent's chess pieces.

New Math Chess focuses on the explanation and applications of four fundamental concepts that govern the feasibility and the success of the book. These are:

- Attachment of Digits to an Operator.
- Partial Values of an Operator.
- Partial Equality of two Partial Values of an Operator.
- Partial Equality of an Operator with its Partial Values.

New Math Chess also introduces a new rule regarding a single Digit piece and a single Operator piece of different owners on a line. This simple rule speeds up the game and proves the critical power of Digits over that of Operators in the game.

New Math Chess provides 20 games with solutions for the readers to practice.

Dr George Ho
May 2020

PREFACE OF THE OLD EDITION OF MATHEMATICAL CHESS

Mathematical chess is a two-player educational and recreational game played on ten *Digit pieces* (0, 1, 2, 3, 4, 5, 6, 7, 8, 9) and six *Operator piece*s (Addition, Subtraction, Multiplication, Division, Power, and Root). The default chessboard is a grid made up of nine vertical and nine horizontal lines equally separated.

A chess piece can move freely on any horizontal or vertical line provided other chess pieces do not obstruct it. A move of a chess piece can result in the removal of the opponent's chess pieces.

Mathematical chess is a very flexible game with *ten or more levels of difficulty*, suitable for all *students at primary and high schools and even for mature people*. Depending on their ages and their years at school, the players can select a level among the existing ones or create new levels suitable for their needs.

Mathematical chess offers many benefits that exist in chess playing (European or Chinese chess) and mathematical learning.

Like chess, mathematical chess teaches many things, including *strategic thinking, problem-solving, memory improvement, decision-making, concentration, perseverance, logic, observation, analysis, and organisational skills*.

Mathematical chess itself also promotes *numerical abilities and mental and speedy calculation*.

In mathematical chess, strategies are set up and exercised not only in the *'Play now!'* phase but also in the *'Prepare now!'* phase.

Like chess, a mathematical chess game is a competition of two players. The competition fosters *interest*, promotes *mental alertness*, challenges all students, and elicits the *highest levels of achievement* (Stephan 1988). [1]

Mathematical chess is an *educational game*. A learning environment organised around games has a positive effect on students' attitudes towards learning. This affective dimension acts as a facilitator of cognitive achievement (Allen and Main 1976). [2]

At the 40th World Chess Congress in 1969, Dr Hans Klaus, dean of the School of Philosophy at Humboldt University in Berlin, commented upon the chess studies completed in Germany:

> Chess helps any human being to elaborate on exact methods of thinking. It would be particularly useful to start playing Chess from the early days … *Everybody prefers to learn something while playing rather than to learn it formally* … it produces in our children an improvement in their school achievements. Those children who received systematic instructions in Chess improved their school efficiency in different subjects, in contrast with those who did not receive that kind of instruction.[3]

I think that the statements of Dr Hans Klaus can also apply to *mathematical chess*.

Dr George Ho
May 2017

---

[1] References in *Teacher's Guide: Research and Benefits of Chess* by Dr Robert C. Fergusion See http://www.quadcitychess.com/benefits_of_chess.html.

[2] Ibid

[3] Ibid

Same Author

Sudoku Training
ISBN 978-1-4251-1318-6, published on June 200 by Trafford Publishing
Order online at www.trafford.com/06-3077
E-mail order: order@ trafford.com

> The book describes the Value and Candidate Rules, the Trial and Error technology of Sudoku, and proposes a logical and systematic resolution of Sudoku puzzles.

Explained Sudoku
ISBN 978-4251-3778-6, published in November 2007 by Trafford Publishing
Order online at ww.trafford.com/07-1504
E-mail order: order@ trafford.com

> The book describes a standard method to logically and systematically solve Sudoku puzzles and applies the method to solve with explanation 30 hard to tough Sudoku puzzles.

Ô Chữ Việt Nam – Quy ước và Thực hành (Vietnamese Crosswords – Conventions and Practices)
ISBN 978-1-4269-1310-5, published in October 2009
Order online at www.trafford.com
E-mail order: order@trafford.com

> The book promotes a specific method to create and solve Vietnamese Crossword puzzles.
> It contains solutions of twelve 7x7 puzzles, twelve 9x9 puzzles, ten 11x11 puzzles, and ten 13x13 puzzles and ten 15x15 puzzles.

Mathematical Chess
ISBN978-1-5434-0163-9, published in July 2019 by Xlibris
Order online at www.Xlibris.com.au
E-mail order: Orders@Xlibris.com.au

> Mathematical Chess is a two-player educational and entertaining game played on ten Digit pieces (0, 1. 2, 3, 4, 5, 6, 7, 8, 9) and six operator

pieces (Addition, subtraction, multiplication, division, power, root). The game has 12 rules played on a chessboard made up of nine vertical and nine horizontal lines equally separated.

Logical Crossnumber Puzzles
ISBN 978-1-7960-0786-2, published in February 2020 by Xlibris
Order online at www.Xlibris.com.au
E-mail order: Orders@Xlibris.com.au

The book enhances the structure and contents of the old Crossnumber puzzles by making their clues more precise, easily and quickly understood, the numbers easily located and relationships between numbers easily formulated.

The book has 50 puzzles of 5 levels of difficulty, covering sophisticated mathematical knowledge, not just simple arithmetical relations between numbers, making the solving of the puzzles more challenging and more useful to the development of the brain and the acquisition of mathematical abilities.

CONTENTS

Preface of New Math Chess vii
Preface of the old edition of Mathematical Chess ix

Chapter 1: New Math Chess Components 1
    Objectives. 1
    Chess Pieces. 1
        Digit pieces.. *1*
        Operator pieces. *2*
    Chessboard... 2
    Chess Pieces on the Chessboard. 3
    Initial display of a standard Math Chess game. 4
    The Time Limit. 4
    Termination of a Math Chess game. 5

Chapter 2: Four fundamental concepts in New Math Chess 7
    1. Attachment of Digits to Operators 7
    2. Partial Values of Operators. 8
        2.1. Partial Sums of Addition. *9*
        2.2. Partial Differences of Subtraction. *9*
        2.3. Partial Products of Multiplication. *10*
        2.4. Partial Quotients of Division. *10*
        2.5. Partial Square/Cube powers of Power. *11*
        2.6. Partial Square/Cube roots of Root. *12*
    3. Single Digit attached to a multi-term Operator............. 13
    4. Partial Equality of Partial Values and
        Partial Equality of Operators. 15
    5. Table of Squares, Cubes, Square Roots, Cube Roots. ... 19
    6. Other New Math Chess Definitions............................... 19
        6.1 Operator Pair. *19*
        6.2 Digit Pair. *20*

Chapter 3: New Math Chess Rules 21
    R01: One Move in turn. 21
    R02: Removal by Operator piece. 21
    R03: Removal by two single Digit pieces on a line. 22
    R04: Removal by single Digit and Operator pieces
        on a line. 22
    R05: Removal by Operator Pair. 23
    R06: Removal by Digit Pair 24
    R07: Removal by Partial Equality of Operator. 25
    R08: Multiple Removals by Operator pieces. 32
    R09: Extended Effect of Operator pieces. 35
    R10: Multiple Removals by Digit pieces. 39
    R11: Extended Effect of Digit pieces. 39
    R12: Removals without moving. 42

The Flexibility of the New Math Chess 44
Conclusion: My Dream 45
Practicing New Match Chess 47
    1. New Math Chess Game 01 - 4 Additions. 47
    2. New Math Chess Game 02 - 4 Subtractions. 48
    3. New Math Chess Game 03 - 4 Multiplications. 50
    4. New Math Chess Game 04 - 4 Divisions. 51
    5. New Math Chess Game 05 – 4 Powers. 53
    6. New Math Chess Game 06 – 4 Roots. 54
    7. New Math Chess Game 07 – 2A2S. 56
    8. New Math Chess Game 08 – 2M2D. 57
    9. New Math Chess Game 09 – 2P2R. 58
    10. New Math Chess Game 10 – 1A1S1M1D. 60
    11. New Math Chess Game 11 – 1A1S1M1D. 61
    12. New Math Chess Game 12 – 1A1S1M1D. 63
    13. New Math Chess Game 13 – 1A1S1M1D. 64
    14. New Math Chess Game 14 – 1A1S1M1D1P1R. 66
    15. New Math Chess Game 15 – 1A1S1M1D1P1R. 67
    16. New Math Chess Game 16 – 1A1S1M1D1P1R. 69
    17. New Math Chess Game 17 – 1A1S1M1D1P1R. 70
    18. New Math Chess Game 18 – 1A1S1M1D1P1R. 72
    19. New Math Chess Game 19 – 1A1S1M1D1P1R. 74
    20. New Math Chess Game 20 – 1A1S1M1D1P1R. 75

List of Definitions, Conventions, Rules 77
About the Author 81

CHAPTER 1

New Math Chess Components

Objectives.

New Math Chess is a two-player educational and recreational game which helps players develop their ability to think ahead, their reasoning and most importantly, their numerical skill, observation and memory.

Chess Pieces.

There are two types of chess pieces: Digit pieces and Operator pieces[4].

Digit pieces.

There are 20 Digit pieces: *0, 1, 2, 3, 4, 5, 6, 7, 8, 9*
(10 Digit pieces for each player)

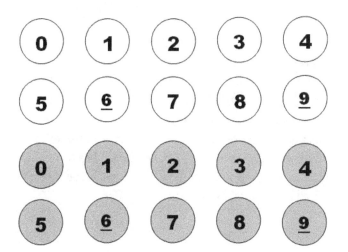

---

[4] These pieces are divided into two sets - one for each player. These sets have different colors: black and white or blue and red for instance.

Operator pieces.

There are 48 Operator pieces for 6 Operators: *Addition, Subtraction, Multiplication, Division, Power (Square/Cube), Root (Square/Cube Root).* (24 Operator pieces for each player)

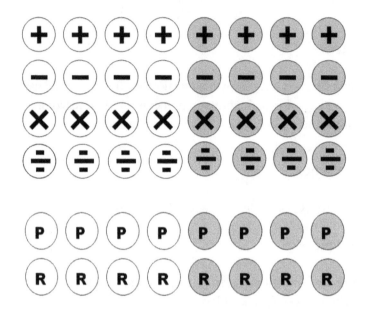

P: Power (Square and Cube),   **R**: Root (Square Root and Cube Root)

Chessboard.

The chessboard is a square grid made up of an equal number of vertical lines and horizontal lines equally separated. The default grid of nine vertical lines and nine horizontal lines, as shown in the following figure, is used throughout this document. The chessboard has 81 nodes, where the chess pieces can reside. Bound by the chess rules, a chess piece can move freely on a line (horizontal or vertical).

NEW MATH CHESS

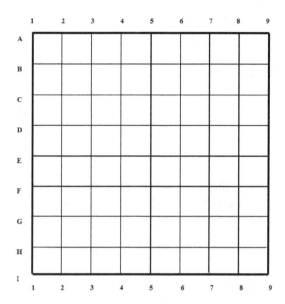

Chess Pieces on the Chessboard.

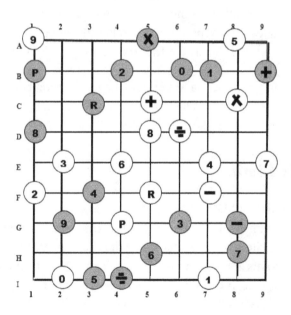

A **standard** New Math Chess game initially has 32 chess pieces on the chessboard. Each player has 16 pieces, including 10 Digit pieces from 0 to

3

9 and 6 Operator pieces, including: Addition, Subtraction, Multiplication, Division, Power (Square/Cube), and Root (Square/Cube Root).

The number of Digit pieces as well as the number and names of the Operators can vary. For training purpose, each player can have only 9 Digit pieces from 1 to 9, and 4 Operator pieces, for examples, 4 Additions, 2 Additions + 2 Subtractions, 4 Multiplications, 2 Multiplications + 2 Divisions, 2 Powers + 2 Roots, …

On the chessboard, the chess pieces can move along the horizontal or vertical chess lines and stop on the nodes of the chessboard.

Initial display of a standard Math Chess game.

For a standard Math Chess game, 32 chess pieces, comprising 20 Digit pieces and 12 Operator pieces, are put in a can. A supervisor (teacher, parent, or one player) shakes the can few times before throwing the chess pieces on the chessboard, then moves the chess pieces to their close nodes on the board. When all chess pieces are on the nodes, the game can begin. If one player does this preparation, the other player starts the first move, otherwise, the white side has the first move.

For educational purposes, a supervisor (teacher, parent) can preset the initial display of the game. The book contains 20 preset New Math Chess games with solutions for the novices to learn and play.

The Time Limit.

The Time Limit of a Math Chess game can be set to 30 minutes if needed. When a Math game ends due to Time Limit, the ranking, if necessary, can be based on the chess pieces remained on the chessboard: 1 point for a Digit piece and 2 points for an Operator piece. The side with the higher total point wins the game. A draw happens if two sides have the same total point.

Termination of a Math Chess game.

A Math Chess game ends when one of the following cases happens:

   a) All Operator pieces of one side were removed, the other side wins the game.
   b) All Digit pieces of one side were removed, the other side wins the game.
   c) The Time Limit has passed.

CHAPTER 2

Four fundamental concepts in New Math Chess

Attachment of Digits to Operators
Partial Values of Operators
Partial Equality of Partial Values
Partial Equality of Operators

1. Attachment of Digits to Operators

<u>**Definition 1:**</u> A Digit attaches to an Operator if it is on the same line (horizontal or vertical) with the Operator and no other Operator exists between them.

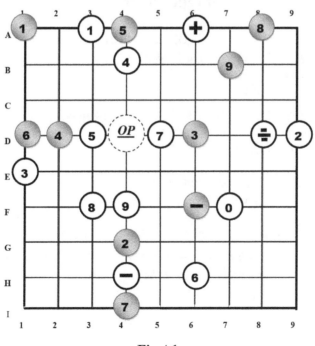

<u>Fig A1</u>

In Fig A1, **OP** represents any Operator piece.

On line D, the Digits Black 6, Black 4 and White 5 attach to the operator **OP** on the left.
The Digits White 7, Black 3 attach to the operator **OP** on the right.
The Digit White 2 doesn't attach to the operator **OP**. It attaches to the White Division.

On line A, the Digits Black 1, White 1, Black 5 and Black 8 attach to the White Addition.
On line F, the Digits White 8, White 9 and White 0 attach to the Black Subtraction.

On column 4, the Digits Black 5, White 4, White 9, and Black 2 attach to the operator **OP**. The Digit Black 7 doesn't attach to the operator **OP**. It attaches to the White Subtraction.

On column 6, the Digits Black 3 and White 6 attach to the Black Subtraction.

2. Partial Values of Operators.

On line D of Fig A1, the Digits Black 6, Black 4 and White 5 attach to the operator **OP** on the left. The Digits White 7, Black 3 attach to the operator **OP** on the right.

The following formula describes these relationships:

    6, 4, 5 (**OP**) 7, 3   (1)

OP is one of six operators: Addition, Subtraction, Multiplication, Division, Power (Square/Cube), Root (Square/Cube Root).

Remark: *'Left' and 'Right' indicate two different sides of an operator. They also cover the cases 'above' and 'below' if the Operator and the Digits are on the same column.*

2.1. Partial Sums of Addition.

***OP* is an Addition:**

(1) => 6, 4, 5 (**+**) 7, 3

6, 4, 5 (+) means "6 + 4 + 5 =" and (+) 7, 3 means "= 7 + 3"

Three Digits 6, 4, 5 generate four partial sums:

6 + 4 + 5 = 15, 6 + 4 = 10, 6 + 5 = 11, 4 + 5 = 9.

Definition 2: The sums 15, 10, 11, 9 are the *left Partial Sums* or the *left Partial Values* of the operator Addition.

Two Digits 7, 3 generate one partial sum: 7 + 3 = 10.

Definition 3: The sum 10 is the *right Partial Sum* or the *right Partial Value* of the operator Addition.

2.2. Partial Differences of Subtraction.

***OP* is a Subtraction.**

(1) => 6, 4, 5 (**−**) 7, 3

6, 4, 5 (−) means "(6 − 4), (4 − 6), (6 − 5), (5 − 6), (4 − 5), (5 − 4) =" and (−) 7, 3 means "= (7 − 3), (3 − 7)"

Convention 1: *Subtraction deals with only two terms. If the first term is less than the second one, increase it by 10.*

Three Digits 6, 4, 5 generate six partial differences:

6 − 4 = 2, (4+10) − 6 = 8, 6 − 5 = 1, (5+10) − 6 = 9,
(4+10) − 5 = 9, 5 − 4 = 1

Definition 4: The differences 2, 8, 1, 9 are the *left Partial Differences* or the *left Partial Values* of the operator Subtraction.

Two Digits 7, 3 generate two partial differences: $7 - 3 = 4$, $(3+10) - 7 = 6$

Definition 5: The differences 4, 6 are the *right Partial Differences* or the *right Partial Values* of the operator Subtraction.

2.3. Partial Products of Multiplication.

***OP* is a Multiplication.**

(1) =>   6, 4, 5 (**X**) 7, 3

6, 4, 5 (**X**) means "6 x 4 x 5 =" and   (**X**) 7, 3 means "= 7 x 3"

Three Digits 6, 4, 5 generate four partial products:

6 x 4 x 5 = 120,   6 x 4 = 24,   6 x 5 = 30,   4 x 5 = 20.

Definition 6:   The products 120, 24, 30, 20 are the *left Partial Products* or the *left Partial Values* of the operator Multiplication.

Two Digits 7, 3 generate one partial product: 7 x 3 = 21.

Definition 7: Product 21 is the *right Partial Product* or the *right Partial Value* of the operator Multiplication.

2.4. Partial Quotients of Division.

***OP* is a Division.**

(1) =>   6, 4, 5 (÷) 7, 3

6, 4, 5 (÷) means "(6 ÷ 4), (4 ÷ 6), (6 ÷ 5), (5 ÷ 6), (4 ÷ 5), (5 ÷ 4) =" and (÷) 7, 3 means "= (7 ÷ 3), (3 ÷ 7)"

Convention 2: *Division deals with only two terms. If a dividend is not divisible by the divisor, increase it by a multiple of 10 so that a one-digit quotient can be obtained.*

Three Digits 6, 4, 5 generate four partial quotients:

$(10+6) \div 4 = 4,$ $(20+4) \div 6 = 4$
$(30+6) \div 4 = 9,$ $(50+4) \div 6 = 9$

Definition 8: The quotients 4 and 9 are the *left Partial Quotients* or the *left Partial Values* of the operator Division.

Two Digits 7, 3 generate two partial quotients:

$(20+7) \div 3 = 9,$ $(60+3) \div 7 = 9$

Definition 9: The quotient 9 is the *right Partial Quotient* or the *right Partial Value* of the operator Division.

Another example: 8, 3, 6 ($\div$) 4, 9

8, 3, 6 ($\div$) means "(8 ÷ 3), (3 ÷ 8), (8 ÷ 6), (6 ÷ 8), (3 ÷ 6), (6 ÷ 3) ="
($\div$) 4, 9 means "= (4 ÷ 9), (9 ÷ 4)"

Three Digits 8, 3, 6 generate six partial quotients:

$(10+8) \div 3 = 6,$ $(10+8) \div 6 = 3,$ $(40+8) \div 6 = 8,$
$(10+6) \div 8 = 2,$ $(50+6) \div 8 = 7,$ $6 \div 3 = 2$

The quotients 8, 7, 6, 3, 2 are the *left Partial Quotients* or *the left Partial Values* of the operator Division.

Two Digits 4, 9 generate only one partial quotient:

$(50+4) \div 9 = 6$

The quotient 6 is the *right Partial Quotient* or *the right Partial Value* of the operator Division.

2.5. Partial Square/Cube powers of Power.

***OP* is a Power (Square/Cube).**

(1) => 6, 4, 5 (**P**) 7, 3

6, 4, 5 (**P**)   means "$6^2, 6^3, 4^2, 4^3, 5^2, 5^3 =$" and
(**P**) 7, 3   means "$= 7^2, 7^3, 3^2, 3^3$"

Power deals with only one term.

Three Digits 6, 4, 5 generate six Square/Cube Powers:

$6^2 = 36$, $6^3 = 216$, $4^2 = 16$, $4^3 = 64$, $5^2 = 25$, $5^3 = 125$

Definition 10: The Powers 36, 216, 16, 64, 25, 125 are the *left Partial Powers* or the *left Partial Values* of the operator Power.

Two Digits 7, 3 generate four Square/Cube Powers:

$7^2 = 49$, $7^3 = 343$, $3^2 = 9$, $3^3 = 27$

Definition 11: The Powers 49, 343, 9, 27 are the *right Partial Powers* or the *right Partial Values* of the operator Power.

2.6. Partial Square/Cube roots of Root.

OP is a Root (Square/Cube Root).

(1) =>   6, 4, 5 (**R**) 7, 3

6, 4, 5 (**R**)   means "$\sqrt{6}, \sqrt[3]{6}, \sqrt{4}, \sqrt[3]{4}, \sqrt{5}, \sqrt[3]{5} =$" and
(**R**) 7, 3   means "$= \sqrt{7}, \sqrt[3]{7}, \sqrt{3}, \sqrt[3]{3}$"

Convention 3: *A multiple of 10 is added to a Digit so that a one-digit square Root or cube Root can be obtained.*

Three Digits 6, 4, 5 generate eight Square/Cube Roots:

$\sqrt{10+6} = 4$, $\sqrt{30+6} = 6$, $\sqrt[3]{210+6} = 6$,
$\sqrt{4} = 2$, $\sqrt{60+4} = 8$, $\sqrt[3]{60+4} = 4$,
$\sqrt{20+5} = 5$, $\sqrt[3]{120+5} = 5$

Definition 12: The square/cube roots 4, 6, 2, 8, 5 are the *left Partial Roots* or the *left Partial Values* of the operator Root.

Two Digits 7, 3 generate two Square/Cube Roots:

$$\sqrt[3]{20+7} = 3, \qquad \sqrt[3]{340+3} = 7$$

Definition 13: The cube roots 3 and 7 are the *right Partial Roots* or the *right Partial Values* of the operator Root.

Another example: 2, 4, 7 (**R**) 9, 1

2, 4, 7 (**R**)   means "$\sqrt{2}, \sqrt[3]{2}, \sqrt{4}, \sqrt[3]{4}, \sqrt{7}, \sqrt[3]{7} =$"   and
(**R**) 9, 1   means "$= \sqrt{9}, \sqrt[3]{9}, \sqrt{1}, \sqrt[3]{1}$"

Three Digits 2, 4, 7 generate five Square/Cube Roots:

$$\sqrt[3]{510+2} = 8, \quad \sqrt{4} = 2, \quad \sqrt{60+4} = 8, \quad \sqrt[3]{60+4} = 4,$$
$$\sqrt[3]{20+7} = 3,$$

The square/cube roots 8, 2, 4, 3 are **the left Partial Roots** or **the left Partial Values of the operator Root.**

Two Digits 9, 1 generate six Square/Cube Roots:

$$\sqrt{9} = 3, \quad \sqrt{40+9} = 7, \quad \sqrt[3]{720+9} = 9,$$

$$\sqrt{1} = 1, \quad \sqrt{80+1} = 9, \quad \sqrt[3]{1} = 1$$

The square/cube roots 3, 7, 9, 1 are **the right Partial Roots** or **the right Partial Values of the operator Root.**

3. Single Digit attached to a multi-term Operator.

The multi-term Operators include: Addition, Subtraction, Multiplication, and Division.

Convention 4: *A single Digit attached to a multi-term Operator is a Partial Value of this Operator.*

Note: Partial Value is a common word for Partial Sum, Partial Difference, Partial Product, Partial Quotient, Partial Power, and Partial Root.

In Fig A1, on line A, the Digit Black 8 is a Partial Value of the operator White Addition.
On line D, the Digit White 2 is a Partial Value of the operator White Division.
On line F, the Digit White 0 is a Partial Value of the operator Black Subtraction.
On column 4, the Digit Black 7 is a Partial Value of the operator White Subtraction.
On column 6, the Digits Black 3 and White 6 are the Partial Values of the operator Black Subtraction.

Note: A single Digit attached to a Power or Root operator is not a Partial Value of these operators.

Other examples:

    White 4, Black 8 (White +) Black 2

=> Left Partial Value of the White Addition is 4+8 = 12
    Right Partial Value of the White Addition is 2.

    White 5, Black 7 (Black -) White 6

=> Left Partial Values of the Black Subtraction are 7-5 = 2 and (5+10) - 7 = 8
    Right Partial Value of the Black Subtraction is 6.

    Black 9 (White **x**) White 6, Black 8

=> Left Partial Value of the White Multiplication is 9.
    Right Partial Value of the White Multiplication is 6 x 8 = 48

    Black 7 (White ÷) White 6

=> Left Partial Value of the White Division is 7
    Right Partial Value of the White Division is 6

4. Partial Equality of Partial Values and Partial Equality of Operators.

Definition 14: Two Partial Values on the same line but different sides of an Operator are *Partially Equal* if they have the *same last Digit*.

Definition 15: The Digits of two equal Partial Values of an Operator and the Operator form a *Partial Equality* of this Operator.

Example 1: Consider the attached Digits and the operator Addition below:

6, 4, 5 (**+**) 7, 3

The left Partial Value $6 + 4 = 10$ and the right Partial Value $7 + 3 = 10$ of the operator Addition have the same last Digit 0

=> These two Partial Values of the operator Addition are Partially Equal.

The Digits 6, 4, 7, 3 of the equal Partial Values and the Operator form a **Partial Equality of Addition:**

6, 4 (**+**) 7, 3

Example 2: Consider the attached Digits and the operator Subtraction below:

6, 4, 3 (**−**) 8, 5

The left Partial Values of the Operator are:

$6 - 4 = 2$, $(4+10) - 6 = 8$, $6 - 3 = 3$, $(3+10) - 6 = 7$
$4 - 3 = 1$, $(3+10) - 4 = 9$

The right Partial Values of the Operator are: $8 - 5 = 3$, $(5+10) - 8 = 7$

The 2 Partial Values $6 - 3 = 3$ and $8 - 5 = 3$ are Partially Equal.

The 2 Partial Values (3+10) – 6 = 7 and (5 +10) – 8 = 7 are Partially Equal.

The Digits 6, 3, 8, 5 of the equal Partial Values and the Operator form a **Partial Equality of Subtraction:**

    6, 3 (–) 8, 5

Example 3:   Consider the attached Digits and the operator Multiplication below.

    8, 4, 2 (**x**) 7, 2, 3

The left Partial Values of the operator are:

    8 x 4 x 2 = 64,   8 x 4 = 32,   8 x 2 = 16,   4 x 2 = 8

The right Partial Values of the operator are:

    7 x 2 x 3 = 42,   7 x 2 = 14,   7 x 3 = 21,   2 x 3 = 6

Two Partial Values 8 x 4 x 2 = 64 and 7 x 2 = 14 are Partially Equal as they have the same last Digit 4.

Two Partial Values 8 x 4 = 32 and 7 x 2 x 3 = 42 are Partially Equal as they have the same last Digit 2.

Two Partial Values 8 x 2 = 16 and 2 x 3 = 6 are Partially Equal as they have the same last Digit 6.

The Digits 8, 4, 2, 7, 2 of the equal Partial Values and the operator form a **Partial Equality of Multiplication:**

    8, 4, 2 (**x**) 7, 2

Similarly, other Partial Equalities of Multiplication are:

    8, 4 (**x**) 7, 2, 3
    8, 2 (**x**) 2, 3

Example 4: Consider the attached Digits of the Operator Division below. 8, 1, 6 (÷) 3, 9

The left Partial Values of the Operator are:

$8 \div 1 = 8$, $(10+8) \div 6 = 3$, $(40+8) \div 6 = 8$,
$(10+6) \div 8 = 2$, $(50+6) \div 8 = 7$, $6 \div 1 = 6$

The right Partial Values of the Operator are: $(60+3) \div 9 = 7$, $9 \div 3 = 3$

Two Partial Values $(10+8) \div 6 = 3$ and $9 \div 3 = 3$ are Partially Equal.
Two Partial Values $(50+6) \div 8 = 7$ and $(60+3) \div 9 = 7$ are Partially Equal.

The Digits 8, 6, 3, 9 of these equal Partial Values and the Operator form a **Partial Equality of Division**:

8, 6 (÷) 3, 9

Example 5: Consider the attached Digits and the operator Power (Square/Cube) as follows:

8, 1, 6 (**P**) 3, 9

The left Partial Values of the Operator are:

$8^2 = 64$, $8^3 = 512$, $1^2 = 1$, $1^3 = 1$, $6^2 = 36$, $6^3 = 216$

The right Partial Values of the Operator are:

$3^2 = 9$, $3^3 = 27$, $9^2 = 81$, $9^3 = 729$

Two Partial Values $1^2 = 1$ and $9^2 = 81$ are Partially Equal.

The Digits 1 and 9 of the equal Partial Values and the Operator form a **Partial Equality of Power:**

1 (**P**) 9

Remark: **a (P) b** with a = b but different owners, is a Partial Equality of Power.

          White 7 **(P)** Black 7   The equal Partial Value is $7^2 = 49$
          Black 9 **(P)** White 9   The equal Partial Value is $9^2 = 81$

Example 6: Consider the attached Digits of the operator Root (Square/Cube Root) below.

    4, 0, 7 **(R)** 2, 9

The left Partial Values of the operator are:

$$\sqrt{4} = 2, \quad \sqrt{60+4} = 8, \quad \sqrt[3]{60+4} = 4,$$
$$\sqrt{0} = 0, \quad \sqrt[3]{0} = 0, \quad \sqrt[3]{20+7} = 3$$

The right Partial Values of the operator are:

$$\sqrt[3]{510+2} = 8, \quad \sqrt{9} = 3, \quad \sqrt{40+9} = 7, \quad \sqrt[3]{720+9} = 9$$

Two Partial Values $\sqrt{60+4} = 8$, and $\sqrt[3]{510+2} = 8$ are Partially Equal.

=> The Digits 4, 2 and the Operator form a **Partial Equality of Root**:

    4 **(R)** 2

Two Partial Values $\sqrt[3]{20+7} = 3$ and $\sqrt{9} = 3$ are Partially Equal.

=> The Digits 7, 9 and the Operator form a Partial Equality of Root:

    7 **(R)** 9

Remark: **a (R) b** with a = b but different owners, is a Partial Equality of Root.

White 1 **(R)** Black 1	The equal Partial Value is $\sqrt{1} = 1$
Black 2 **(R)** White 2	The equal Partial Value is $\sqrt[3]{510+2} = 8$
Black 3 **(R)** White 3	The equal Partial Value is $\sqrt[3]{340+3} = 7$
White 4 **(R)** Black 4	The equal Partial Value is $\sqrt{4} = 2$

Black 5 (**R**) White 5   The equal Partial Value is $\sqrt{20+5} = 5$
White 6 (**R**) Black 6   The equal Partial Value is $\sqrt{10+6} = 4$
Black 7 (**R**) White 7   The equal Partial Value is $\sqrt[3]{20+7} = 3$
Black 8 (**R**) White 8   The equal Partial Value is $\sqrt[3]{8} = 2$
White 9 (**R**) White 9   The equal Partial Value is $\sqrt{9} = 3$

5. Table of Squares, Cubes, Square Roots, Cube Roots.

N	1	2	3	4	5	6	7	8	9
N^2	1	4	9	16	25	36	49	64	81
N^3	1	8	27	64	125	216	343	512	729

N	1	2	3	4	5
$\sqrt{}$	$\sqrt{1}=1$; $\sqrt{(80+1)}=9$			$\sqrt{4}=2$; $\sqrt{(60+4)}=8$	$\sqrt{(20+5)}=5$
$\sqrt[3]{}$	$\sqrt[3]{1}=1$	$\sqrt[3]{(510+2)}=8$	$\sqrt[3]{(340+3)}=7$	$\sqrt[3]{(60+4)}=4$	$\sqrt[3]{(120+5)}=5$

N	6	7	8	9
$\sqrt{}$	$\sqrt{(10+6)}=4$; $\sqrt{(30+6)}=6$			$\sqrt{9}=3$; $\sqrt{(40+9)}=7$
$\sqrt[3]{}$	$\sqrt[3]{(210+6)}=6$	$\sqrt[3]{(20+7)}=3$	$\sqrt[3]{8}=2$	$\sqrt[3]{(720+9)}=9$

$0^2 = 0$, $0^3 = 0$, $\sqrt{0}=0$ $\sqrt[3]{0}=0$

6. Other New Math Chess Definitions.

6.1 Operator Pair.

<u>**Definition 16:**</u> Two Operator pieces of the same player form an *Operator Pair* when they are on the same line (horizontal or vertical) and not separated by any Digit or Operator piece of any player.

Examples:

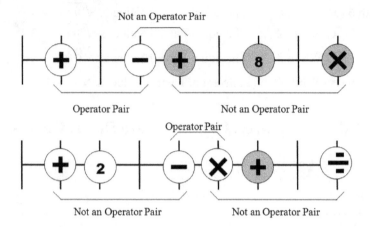

6.2 Digit Pair.

Definition 17: Two Digit pieces of the same player form a *Digit Pair* when they are on the same line (horizontal or vertical) and not separated by any Digit or Operator piece of any player.

Examples:

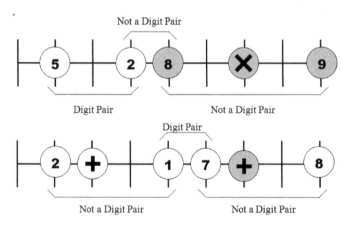

CHAPTER 3

New Math Chess Rules

The New Math Chess games are played based on the following rules:

R01: One Move in turn.
The players, in turn, can move their chess pieces on the chessboard. There is at most **one move in turn.**

A chess piece can move freely along a vertical or horizontal line if other chess pieces do not obstruct the move. The move is not mandatory. The player can remove the opponent's chess pieces without moving any of his or her chess pieces.

R02: Removal by Operator piece.
An Operator piece, when moving along a line, can remove the first opponent's Digit piece or Operator piece it encounters provided *they are different.*

Examples:

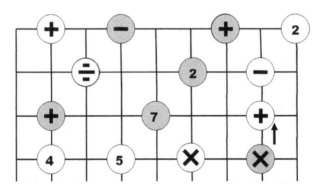

a) On the first horizontal line, the White Addition can remove the Black Subtraction operator. After this move, the Black Addition *cannot* remove the White Addition, but it can remove the White Digit 2.

b) On the eighth vertical line, the Black Multiplication can remove the White Addition. Note that it *cannot* continue removing the White Subtraction (Rule 1). On the contrary, the White Subtraction can remove the Black Multiplication.

c) On the second vertical line, the Black Addition cannot remove the White Addition operator, but it can remove the White Digit 4.

d) On the fourth horizontal line, the White Multiplication cannot remove the Black Multiplication, but it can remove the Black Digit 2 on the vertical line 6.

e) On the fourth vertical line, the Black Subtraction can remove the white Digit 5. After this move, the White Multiplication can remove it.

R03: Removal by two single Digit pieces on a line.

When on a line (horizontal or vertical), there are **only two Digit pieces** of different players, one Digit piece can remove the other provided *they are different*.

Example:

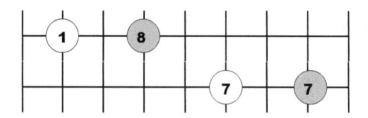

The White Digit 1 can remove the Black Digit 8 and vice versa.
The White Digit 7 *cannot* remove the Black Digit 7 and vice versa.

R04: Removal by single Digit and Operator pieces on a line.

When on a line (horizontal or vertical), there are **only one Digit piece and one Operator piece** of different players. The Digit piece can also remove the Operator piece.

Example:

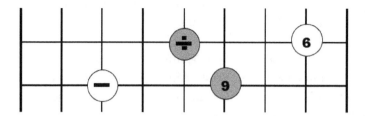

The Black Division can remove the White Digit 6, and the White Subtraction can remove the Black Digit 9.   (Rule 1).
The White Digit 6 can remove the Black Division, and the Black Digit 9 can remove the White Subtraction.   (Rule 4).

R05: Removal by Operator Pair.
When on a line (horizontal or vertical), there is an Operator Pair, then one Operator of the pair can jump over its partner and removes any opponent's first Digit or Operator piece situated on the other side. Note that the Operator removed, if any, must be *different* from the jumping Operator.

Examples:

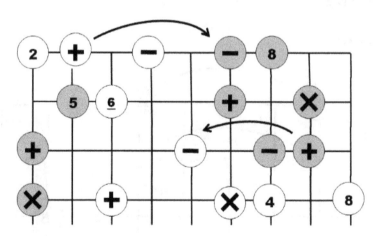

a) On the first line, the White Addition and White Subtraction form an Operator Pair. The White Addition can jump over the White Subtraction to remove the Black Subtraction.

b) On the third line, the Black Addition and Black Subtraction form an Operator Pair. The Black Addition can jump over the Black Subtraction to remove the White Subtraction.

c) On the fourth line, the White Multiplication and White Addition form an Operator Pair. The White Multiplication *cannot* jump over the White Addition to remove the same Black Multiplication, but the White Addition can remove the Black Multiplication.

d) On the second line, the Black Multiplication and Black Addition form an Operator Pair. If the Black Multiplication jumps over the Black Addition and removes the White Digit 6, it is removed later by the White Addition on line 4. The best way is removing the White Digit 6 by the Black Addition.

R06: Removal by Digit Pair

When on a line (horizontal or vertical), there is a Digit Pair, then one Digit of the pair can jump over its partner to remove any opponent's first Digit or Operator piece situated on the other side.

Note that the Digit piece removed, if any, *must be different* from the jumping Digit.

Examples:

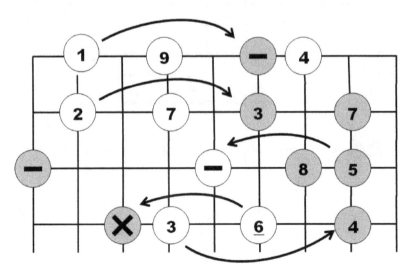

a) On the first line, White Digit 1 and White Digit 9 form a Digit Pair. White Digit 1 can jump over its partner White Digit 9 to remove Black Subtraction.

b) On the second line, Black Digit 3 and Black Digit 7 form a Digit Pair. Black Digit 7 *cannot* jump over Black Digit 3 to remove the White Digit 7 as they have the same value. On the contrary, White Digit 2 can jump over White Digit 7 to remove Black Digit 3.

c) On the third line, Black Digit 5 and Black Digit 8 form a Digit Pair. Black Digit 5 can jump over its partner Black Digit 8 to remove White Subtraction.

d) On the fourth line, White Digit 3 and White Digit 6 form a Digit Pair. White Digit 6 can jump over its partner White Digit 3 to remove Black Multiplication or White Digit 3 can jump over White Digit 6 to remove Black Digit 4.

R07: Removal by Partial Equality of Operator.

If a side moves a chess piece (Digit or Operator) to a new position that results in a Partial Equality of any Operator, it can remove any opponent's chess piece (Digit or Operator) in this Partial Equality.

There are 6 types of Partial Equality of 6 operators: Addition, Subtraction, Multiplication, Division, Power, and Root.

Example 1a: Partial Equality of Addition.

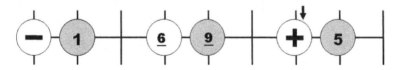

The *arrow* indicates the movement direction of the chess piece.

The white side moves its White Addition to a position that creates a Partial Equality of Addition:

White 6, Black 9 (*White +*) Black 5

=> The White Addition removes 2 opponent's chess pieces: Black 9 and Black 5.

Example 1b: Partial Equality of Addition.

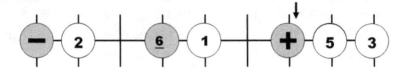

The black side moves its Black Addition to a position that creates a Partial Equality of Addition:

   White 2, Black 6 (***Black +***) White 5, White 3

=> The Black Addition removes 3 opponent's chess pieces: White 2, White 5 and White 3.

Example 1c: Partial Equality of Addition.

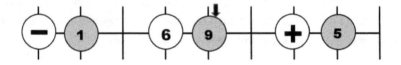

The black side moves its Black Digit 9 to a position that creates a Partial Equality of Addition:

   White 6, ***Black 9*** (White **+**) Black 5

=> The Black Digit 9 removes 2 opponent's chess pieces: White 6 and White Addition.

Example 2a: Partial Equality of Subtraction.

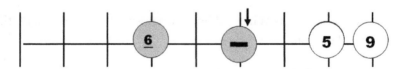

The black side moves its Black Subtraction to a position that creates a Partial Equality of Subtraction:

Black 6 (***Black* -**) White 5, White 9   as 6 and (5+10) − 9 = 6

=> The Black Subtraction removes 2 opponent's chess pieces: White 5 and White 9.

Example 2b: Partial Equality of Subtraction.

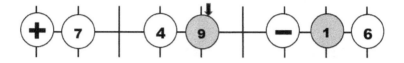

The black side moves its black Digit 9 to a position that creates a Partial Equality of Subtraction:

White 4, ***Black 9*** (White -) Black 1, White 6

=> The black Digit 9 removes 3 opponent's chess pieces: White 4, White 6 and White Subtraction.

Example 3a: Partial Equality of Multiplication.

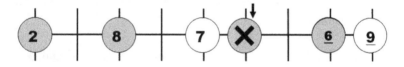

The black side moves its Black Multiplication to a position that creates a Partial Equality of Multiplication:

Black 2, White 7 (***Black* x**) Black 6, White 9   as 2x7 = 14 and 6x9 = 54

=> The Black Multiplication removes 2 opponent's chess pieces: White 7 and White 9.

Example 3b: Partial Equality of Multiplication.

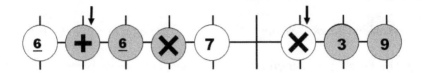

A move of the Black Addition (+) can remove the white Digit 6.

A move of the White Multiplication generates the Partial Equality of Multiplication:

   White 7 (***White* x**) Black 3, Black 9

=> The White Multiplication removes 2 opponent's chess pieces: Black 3 and Black 9.

Example 3c: Partial Equality of Multiplication.

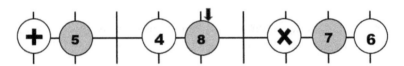

The black side moves its Black Digit 8 to a position that creates a Partial Equality of Multiplication:

   White 4, ***Black 8*** (White **x**) Black 7, White 6   as 4x8 = 32 and 7x6 = 42

=> The black Digit 8 removes 3 opponent's chess pieces: White 4, White 6 and White Multiplication.

Example 4a: Partial Equality of Division.

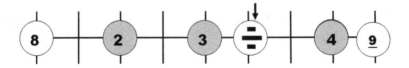

The white side moves its White Division to a position that creates a Partial Equality of Division:

White 8, Black 3 (***White*** ÷) Black 4, White 9

as $(10+8) \div 3 = 6$ and $(50+4) \div 9 = 6$

=> The White Division removes 2 opponent's chess pieces: Black 3 and Black 4.

Example 4b: Partial Equality of Division.

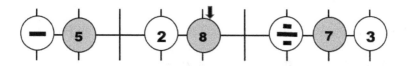

The black side moves its Black Digit 8 to a position that creates a Partial Equality of Division:

White 2, ***Black 8*** (White ÷) Black 7, White 3

as $(10 + 8) \div 2 = 9$ and $(20 + 7) \div 3 = 9$

=> The black Digit 8 removes 3 opponent's chess pieces: White 2, White 3 and White Division.

Example 5a: Partial Equality of Power (Square/Cube)

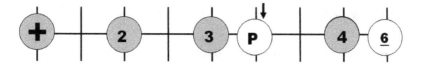

The white side moves its White Power to a position that creates a Partial Equality of Power:

Black 2 (***White* P**) Black 4   as $2^2 = 4$ and $4^3 = 64$

=> The White Power removes 2 opponent's chess pieces: Black 2 and Black 4.

Example 5b: Partial Equality of Power.

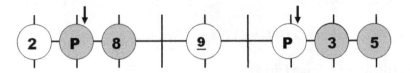

A move of the Black Power operator creates a Partial Equality of Power:

    White 2 (***Black* P**) Black 8   as $2^2 = 4$ and $8^2 = 64$

=> The Black Power removes the opponent's chess piece: White 2.

A move of the White Power creates the Partial Equality of Power:

    White 9 (***White* P**) Black 3   as $9^3 = 729$ and $3^2 = 9$

=> The White Power removes the opponent's chess piece: Black 3.

Example 5c: Partial Equality of Power.

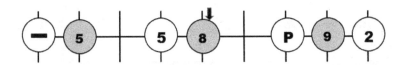

The black side moves its Black Digit 8 to a position that creates a Partial Equality of Power:

    ***Black* 8** (White P) White 2   as $8^2 = 64$ and $2^2 = 4$

=> The Black Digit 8 removes 2 opponent's chess pieces: White 2 and White Power.

Example 6a: Partial Equality of Root (Square/Cube root)

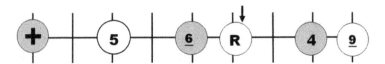

The white side moves its White Root to a position that creates a Partial Equality of Root:

Black 6 (**White R**) Black 4   as $\sqrt{10+6} = 4$ and $\sqrt[3]{60+4} = 4$

=> The White Root removes 2 opponent's chess pieces: Black 6, Black 4.

Example 6b: **Partial Equality of Root.**

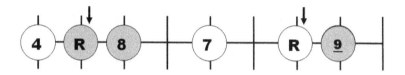

A move of the Black Root creates a Partial Equality of Root:

White 4 (**Black R**) Black 8   as $\sqrt{4} = 2$ and $\sqrt[3]{8} = 2$

=> The Black Root removes the opponent's chess piece: White 4.

A move of the White Root creates a Partial Equality of Root:

White 7 (**White R**) Black 9   as $\sqrt[3]{20+7} = 3$ and $\sqrt{9} = 3$

=> The White Root removes the opponent's chess piece: Black 9.

Example 6c: **Partial Equality of Root.**

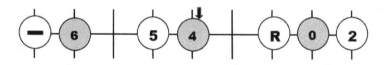

The black side moves its black Digit 4 to a position that creates a Partial Equality of Root:

Black 4 (White R) White 2   as $\sqrt{60+4} = 8$ and $\sqrt[3]{510+2} = 8$

=> The Black Digit 4 removes 2 opponent's chess pieces: White 2 and White Root.

R08: Multiple Removals by Operator pieces.

The move of an Operator can create more than one different Partial Equalities which trigger multiple removals of opponent's Digits.

An Operator can deny removing any opponent's Digit piece for its subsequent removals.

Example 1:

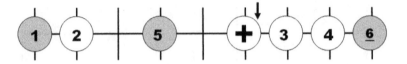

The white side moves its White Addition to a position that creates 2 Partial Equalities of Addition:

   Black 1, White 2 (*White* +) White 3, White 4, Black 6

=> The White Addition removes Black 1, Black 6.

   White 2, Black 5 (*White* +) White 3, White 4

=> The White Addition removes Black 5.

In total, the White Addition removes 3 opponent's chess pieces: Black 1, Black 6, and Black 5.

Example 2:

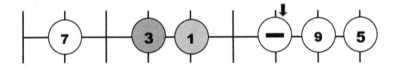

The white side moves its White Subtraction to a position that creates 2 Partial Equalities of Subtraction:

   White 7, Black 3 (*White* -) White 9, White 5

=> The White Subtraction removes Black 3.

   White 7, Black 1 (***White*** -) White 9, White 5

   as 7−1 = 6 and (10+5) − 9 = 6

=> The White Subtraction removes Black 1.

In total, the White Subtraction removes 2 opponent's chess pieces: Black 3 and Black 1.

Example 3:

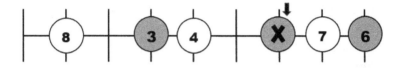

The black side moves its Black Multiplication to a position that creates 2 Partial Equalities of Multiplication:

   Black 3, White 4 (***Black*** ×) White 7, Black 6   as 3x4 = 12, 7x6 = 42

=> The Black Multiplication removes White 4, White 7.

   White 8, White 4 (***Black*** ×) White 7, Black 6   as 8x4 = 32, 7x6 = 42

=> The Black Multiplication removes White 8.

In total, the Black Multiplication removes 3 opponent's chess pieces: White 4, White 7, and White 8.

Example 4:

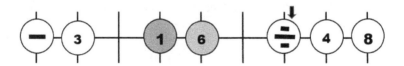

The white side moves its White Division to a position that creates 2 Partial Equalities of Division:

    White 3, Black 6 (***White*** ÷) White 4, White 8 as 6 ÷ 3 = 2 and 8 ÷ 4 = 2

=> The White Division removes Black 6.

    White 3, Black 1 (***White*** ÷) White 4, White 8

    as 3 ÷ 1 = 3 and (20+4) ÷ 8 = 3

=> The White Division removes Black 1.

In total, the White Division removes 2 opponent's chess pieces: Black 6 and Black 1.

Example 5:

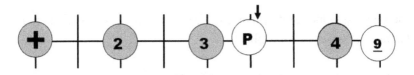

The white side moves its White Power to a position that creates 2 Partial Equalities for Power:

    Black 2 (***White* P**) Black 4   as $2^2 = 4$, $4^3 = 64$

=> The White Power removes Black 2, Black 4.

    Black 3 (***White* P**) White 9   as $3^2 = 9$, $9^3 = 729$

=> The White Power removes Black 3.

In total, the White Power removes 3 opponent's chess pieces: Black 2, Black 4, and Black 3.

Example 6:

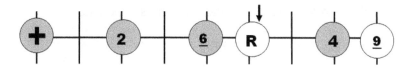

The white side moves its White Root to a position that creates 2 Partial Equalities of Root:

Black 6 (***White* R**) Black 4   as $\sqrt{10+6} = 4$ and $\sqrt[3]{60+4} = 4$

=> The White Root removes Black 6, Black 4.

Black 2 (***White* R**) Black 4   as $\sqrt[3]{510+2} = 8$ and $\sqrt{60+4} = 8$

=> The White Root removes Black 2.

In total, the White Root removes 3 opponent's chess pieces: Black 6, Black 4, Black 2

R09: Extended Effect of Operator pieces.
The effect of an Operator piece remains after it removes the opponent's Digits, i.e. the Operator piece can continue removing the opponent's Digits if it satisfies other conditions.

An Operator piece can deny removing any opponent's Digit piece for its subsequent removals.

Example 1:

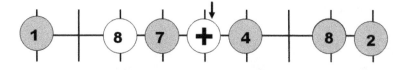

The move of the White Addition to its position creates a Partial Equality of Addition:

Black 1, White 8, Black 7 (*White* +) Black 4, Black 2

=> The White Addition removes the opponent's chess pieces:

Black 1, Black 7, Black 4 and Black 2.

After these removals, the remaining chess pieces on the line are as follows:

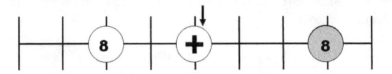

"White 8 (*White* +) Black 8" is a Partial Equality of the White Addition, causing the removal of the Black 8.

In total, the White Addition removes 5 opponent's chess pieces: Black 1, Black 7, Black 4, Black 2, and Black 8.

Example 2:

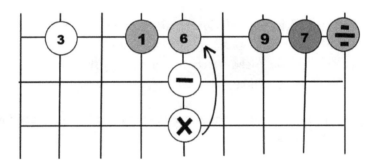

The White Multiplication jumps over its partner, the White Subtraction, to remove Black 6.

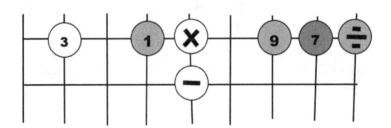

At its new position, the while Multiplication creates a Partial Equality of Multiplication:

White 3, Black 1 (***White* x**) Black 9, Black 7 as 3 x 1 = 3 and 9 x 7 = 63

=> Black 1, Black 9, Black 7 removed.

In total, the White Multiplication removes 4 opponent's chess pieces: Black 6, Black 1, Black 9, and Black 7.

Example 3:

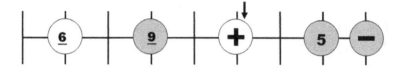

The move of the White Addition to its position creates a Partial Equality of Addition:

White 6, Black 9 (***White* +**) Black 5

=> Black 9, Black 5 removed

After these removals, the remaining chess pieces on the line are as follows:

The White Addition *cannot* remove the Black Subtraction because only one move is allowed in turn (Rule 1). On the contrary, the Black Subtraction can remove the White Addition. To avoid this case, the White Addition should not remove Black 5.

Example 4:

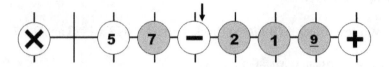

The move of the White Subtraction to its position creates a Partial Equality of Subtraction:

> White 5, Black 7 (***White* -**) Black 1, Black 9
> as $(10 + 5) - 7 = 8$ and $9 - 1 = 8$

=> The White Subtraction removes the opponent's chess pieces: Black 7, Black 1, and Black 9.

To also remove Black 2, the White Subtraction shouldn't remove Black 7. The remaining chess pieces on the line are as follows:

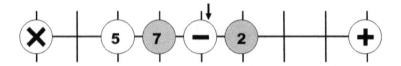

The Partial Equality "White 5, Black 7 (***White* -**) Black 2" results in the removal of Black 7 and Black 2.

Example 5:

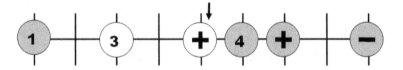

The move of the White Addition to its position creates a Partial Equality of Addition:

> Black 1, White 3 (***White* +**) Black 4

=> Black 1, Black 4 removed

However, if Black 4 removed, Black Subtraction jumps over its partner Black Addition to remove White Addition.

So, the White Addition shouldn't remove Black 4.

R10: Multiple Removals by Digit pieces.
A move of a Digit piece can result in many Partial Equalities of the same or different Operators.

Example 1:

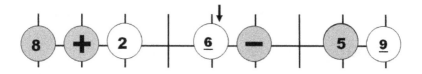

The move of White Digit 6 to its position creates 2 Partial Equalities: one of Addition and one of Subtraction:

   Black 8 (Black +) White 2, *White 6*

=> White Digit 6 removes Black 8 and Black Addition.

   White 2, *White 6* (Black -) Black 5, White 9

=> White Digit 6 removes Black 5 and Black Subtraction.

In total, White Digit 6 removes 4 opponent's chess pieces: Black 8, Black 5, Black Addition and Black Subtraction.

R11: Extended Effect of Digit pieces.
The effect of a Digit piece remains after it removes the opponent's Digit and Operator pieces – i.e. the Digit piece can continue removing the opponent's Digit and Operator pieces if it satisfies other conditions.

A Digit piece can deny removing any opponent's Digit piece for its subsequent removals.

Example 1:

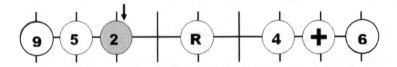

The move of the Black Digit 2 to its position creates the following Partial Equality of Root:

Black 2 (White **R**) White 4 $\quad$ as $\sqrt[3]{510+2} = 8$ and $\sqrt{60+4} = 8$

=> The Digit Black 2 removes Digit White 4 and Operator White Root.

After these removals, the chess pieces remained on the line are:

The new position of Black Digit 2 creates another Partial Equality of Addition:

White 9, White 5, **Black 2** (White +) White 6

=> The Digit Black 2 removes the Digits: While 9, White 5, White 6, and Operator: White Addition.

In total, the Digit Black 2 removes 6 opponent's chess pieces: Digits: White 4, White 9, White 5, White 6, and Operators: White Root, White Addition.

Example 2:

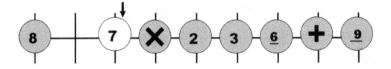

The move of Digit White 7 to its position creates a Partial Equality of Multiplication:

Black 8, *White 7* (Black **x**) Black 2, Black 3, Black 6
as 8 x 7 = 56 and 2 x 3 x 6 = 36

=> The Digit White 7 removes 5 opponent's chess pieces: Digits: Black 8, Black 2, Black 3, Black 6, and Operator: Black Multiplication.

For another removal, the white side should not remove the black Digit 2, and the chess pieces remained on the line are:

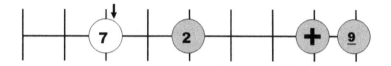

"*White 7*, Black 2 (Black **+**) Black 9" is a Partial Equality of Addition.

=> The Digit White 7 removes Black 2, Black 9, Black Addition.

In total, the Digit White 7 removes 7 opponent's chess pieces: Digits: Black 8, Black 3, Black 6, Black 2, Black 9, and Operators: Black Multiplication, Black Addition.

Example 3:

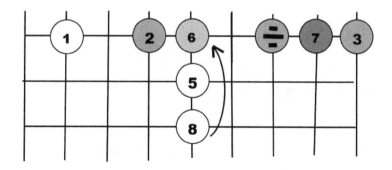

The Digit White 8 jumps over its partner, Digit White 5, to remove Digit Black 6.

=> Black 6 removed.

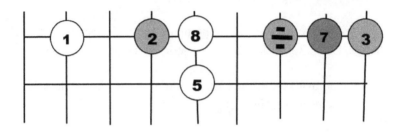

At its new position, Digit While 8 creates a Partial Equality of Division:

Black 2, **White 8** (Black ÷) Black 7, Black 3
as $(10 + 8) \div 2 = 9$ and $(20 + 7) \div 3 = 9$

=> Black 2, Black 7, Black 3, Black Division removed.

In total, the Digit White 8 removes 5 opponent's chess pieces: Digits: Black 6, Black 2, Black 7, Black 3, and Operator: Black Division.

R12: Removals without moving.
A player can remove the opponent's chess pieces without moving any of his or her Digit or Operator pieces.

Example 1:

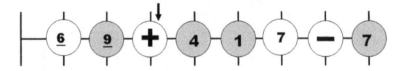

The white side moves its White Addition to a position that creates the following Partial Equality of Addition:

White 6, Black 9 (**White** +) Black 4, Black 1

=> Black 9, Black 4, Black 1 removed

After these removals, the chess pieces remained on the line are:

After these removals of the white side, the black side finds that it faces the following Partial Equality of Subtraction:

White 7 (White -) **Black 7**   => White 7, White Subtraction removed.

Without moving any black chess piece, Black Digit 7 can remove Digit White 7 and Operator White Subtraction.

Example 2:

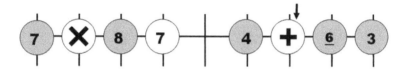

The white side moves its White Addition to a position that creates the following Partial Equality of Addition:

Black 8, White 7, Black 4 *(White +)* Black 6, Black 3
as 8 + 7 + 4 = 19 and 6 + 3 = 9

=> Black 8, Black 4, Black 6, Black 3 removed.

After these removals, the chess pieces remained on the line are:

Without moving any chess piece, Black Digit 7 can remove Digit White 7 and Operator White Multiplication.

The Flexibility of the New Math Chess

New Math Chess offers many flexible choices to make it compatible with the level of knowledge of the players, such as the following:

1. Free to choose the dimension of the chessboard
2. Free to select the conditions of the game:

    a) Inclusion or exclusion of the Digit piece 0
    b) Number of Digit pieces
    c) Number and values of Operator pieces

3. Free to create new levels of difficulty for the game
4. Free to set up a Time Limit for the game.

CONCLUSION

My Dream

With the invention of the New Math Chess, its creator aims at providing a means – a weapon – to separate young people at all levels from their deep passion for electronic games, which has damaged their minds with hatred of mathematics.

To be successful, the New Math Chess needs initial support from people of educational organisations at all levels, from universities to middle and high schools, in such activities as:

1. Distributing the book and explaining the essential rules of New Math Chess.
2. Organising competitions between students in a class and between students in different classes, different schools…
3. Organising yearly competitions between schools in states.

I hope that, eventually, the New Math Chess can fulfil its objectives. My dream is to see the New Math Chess becoming a popular game in all middle and high schools and to see the love and passion of mathematics flowering in the minds of young people around the world.

PRACTICING NEW MATCH CHESS

In all following New Math Chess Games, the White side always goes first. The given solutions are not unique. The author proposes the readers to find out other better solutions. For the sake of simplicity, the words Digit and Operator are not mentioned in this section.

1. New Math Chess Game 01 - 4 Additions.

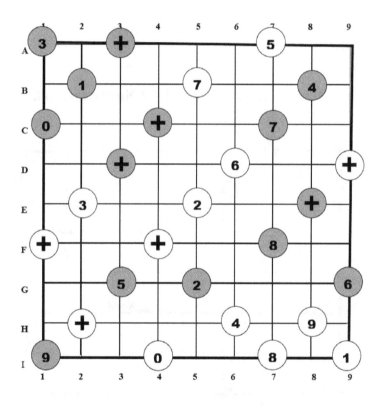

W: White 3 at E2 jumps over its partner White 2 at E5 to remove Black Addition at E8.

B: Black 3 at A1 jumps over its partner Black 0 at C1 to remove White Addition at F1.

W: White 5 at A7 removes Black Addition at A3.

At this new position, White 5 removes Black 5 at G3 and Black Addition at D3.

("***White 5*** (Black +) Black 5" is a Partial Equality of Addition.)

B: Black 1 at B2 removes White Addition at H2.

W: White Addition at F4 removes Black 3 at F1.

B: Black Addition at C4 removes White 0 at I4.

W: White 1 at I9 jumps over its partner White 8 at I7 to remove Black Addition at I4.

Game is over. All Black Additions removed and the White side wins the game.

2. New Math Chess Game 02 - 4 Subtractions.

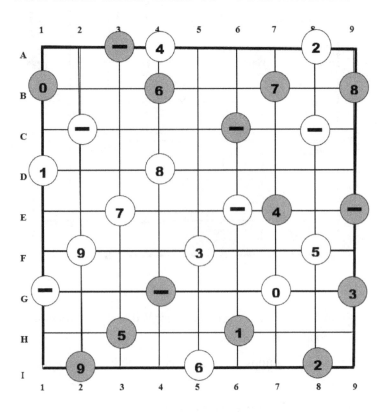

W: White 2 at A8 jumps over its partner White 4 at A4 to remove Black Subtraction at A3.

B: Black 0 at B1 moves to B2 to remove White 9 at F2 and White Subtraction at C2.

("***Black 0*** (White -) White 9, Black 9" is a Partial Equality of Subtraction).

W: White 5 at F8 moves to F9 to remove Black 8 at B9, Black 3 at G9 and Black Subtraction at E9.

("Black 8 (Black -) ***White 5***, Black 3" is a Partial Equality of Subtraction as 8 and (10+3) − 5 = 8 are two equal Partial Values of the Subtraction).

B: Black 2 at I8 removes White Subtraction at C8.

W: White 6 at I5 moves to I4 to remove Black Subtraction at G4.

("***White 6*** (Black -) White 4, White 8" is a Partial Equality of Subtraction as 6 and (10+4) − 8 = 6 are two equal Partial Values of the Subtraction).

B: Black Subtraction at C6 moves to C4 to remove White 4 at A4, White 8 at D4, and White 6 at I4.

("White 4, Black 6 (***Black*** -) White 8, White 6" is a Partial Equality of Subtraction).

W: White 7 at E3 moves to C3.

B: Black Subtraction at C4 removes White 7 at C3.

W: White 3 at F5 moves to F3 to remove Black 5 at H3 and Black Subtraction at C3.

("White 2 (Black -) ***White 3***, Black 5" is a Partial Equality of Subtraction).

Game is over. All Black Subtractions removed and the White side wins the game.

3. New Math Chess Game 03 - 4 Multiplications.

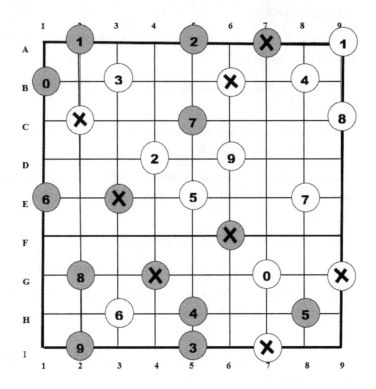

W: White 2 at D4 removes Black Multiplication at G4.

B: Black 6 at E1 moves to C1 to remove White 8 at C9 and White Multiplication at C2.

("***Black 6*** (White x) Black 7, White 8" is a Partial Equality of Multiplication).

W: White 7 at E8 jumps over its partner White 5 at E5 to remove Black Multiplication at E3.

B: Black 9 at I2 jumps over its partner Black 3 at I5 to remove White Multiplication at I7.

W: White Multiplication at B6 moves to B5 to remove Black 2 at A5, Black 4 at H5, and Black 3 at I5.

("Black 2 (***White* x**) Black 4, Black 3" is a Partial Equality of Multiplication).

B: Black Multiplication at F6 removes White 9 at D6.
W: White 5 at E5 moves to E6.
B: Black 7 at C5 removes White Multiplication at B5.
W: White 5 at E6 removes Black Multiplication at D6
B: Black 5 at H8 removes White 4 at B8.
W: White 6 at H3 moves to I3.
B: Black 9 at I7 removes White 6 at I3.
W: White 0 at G7 removes Black Multiplication at A7.

Game is over. All Black Multiplications removed and the White side wins the game.

4. New Math Chess Game 04 - 4 Divisions.

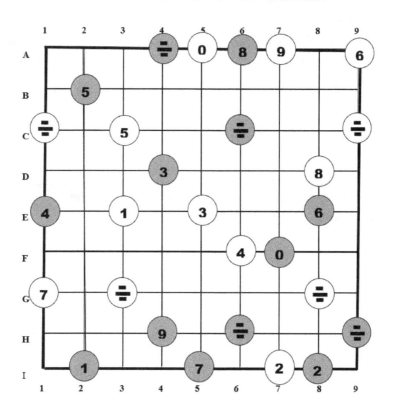

W: White 3 at E5 moves to E6 to remove Black 8 at A6 and Black Division at C6.

("Black 8 (Black ÷) ***White 3***, White 4" is a Partial Equality of Division as 8 and (20+4) ÷ 3 = 8 are two equal Partial Values of the Division)

B: Black 6 at E8 moves to E9 to remove White 6 at A9 and White Division at C9.

("***Black 6*** (White ÷) White 6" is a Partial Equality of Division).

W: White 3 at E6 jumps over its partner White 4 at F6 to remove Black Division at H6.

B: Black 6 at E9 moves to E8 to remove White 8 at D8 and White Division at G8.

("White 8, ***Black 6*** (White ÷) Black 2" is a Partial Equality of Division as 2 and (10+6) ÷ 8 = 2 are two equal Partial Values of the Division).

W: White 9 at A7 jumps over its partner White 0 at A5 to remove Black Division at A4.

B: Black 7 at I5 moves to G5 to remove White 7 at G1 and White Division at G3.

W: White 0 at A5 moves to A9.

B: Black 4 at E1 removes White Division at C1.

Game is over. All White Divisions removed and the Black side wins the game.

5. New Math Chess Game 05 – 4 Powers.

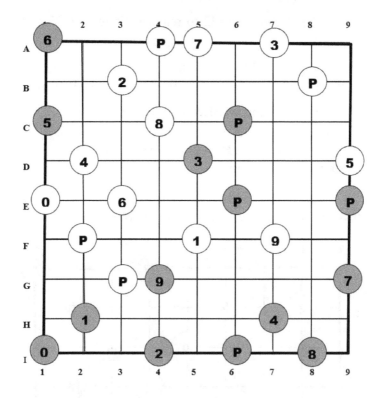

W: White 0 at E1 jumps over its partner White 6 at E3 to remove Black Power at E6.

B: Black 8 at I8 removes White Power at B8.

W: White 3 at A7 moves to A9 to remove Black 7 at G9 and Black Power at E9.

("*White 3* (Black P) Black 7" is a Partial Equality of Power as $3^2 = 9$ and $7^2 = 49$ are two equal Partial Values of the Power).

B: Black 2 at I4 moves to I3 to remove White 2 at B3 and White Power at G3.

("*Black 2* (White P) White 2" is a Partial Equality of Power).

W: White 5 at D9 moves to C9 to remove Black 5 at C1 and Black Power it C6.

("***White 5*** (Black P) Black 5" is a Partial Equality of Power).

B: Black 2 at I3 moves to I2 to remove White 4 at D2 and White Power at F2.

("***Black 2*** (White P) White 4" is a Partial Equality of Power as $2^2 = 4$ and $4^3 = 64$ are two equal Partial Values of the Power).

W: White 0 at E6 removes Black Power at I6.

Game is over. All Black Powers removed and the White side wins the game.

6. New Math Chess Game 06 – 4 Roots.

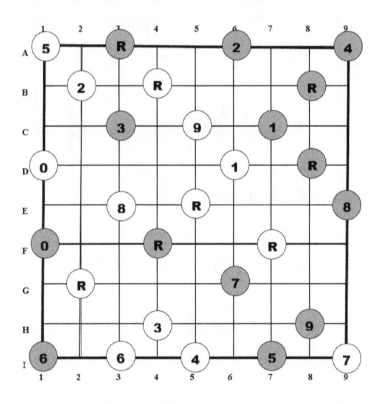

W: White 9 at C5 moves to C4 to remove Black Root at F4.

("***White 9*** (Black R) White 3" is a Partial Equality of Root as $\sqrt{40+9} = 7$, $\sqrt[3]{340+3} = 7$ are two equal Partial Values of the Root).

B: Black 2 at A6 moves to A5 to remove White 4 at I5 and White Root at E5.

("**Black 2** (White R) White 4" is a Partial Equality of Root as $\sqrt[3]{510+2} = 8$, $\sqrt{60+4} = 8$ are two equal Partial Values of the Root).

W: White 2 at B2 moves to A2 to remove Black 2 at A5, Black 4 at A9, and Black Root at A3.

("**White 2** (Black R) Black 2" and "**White 2** (Black R) Black 4" are two Partial Equalities of Power as $\sqrt[3]{510+2} = 8$, $\sqrt{60+4} = 8$ are two equal Partial Values of the Root).

B: Black 7 at G6 removes White Root at G2.

W: White 0 at D1 jumps over is partner White 1 at D6 to remove Black Root at D8.

B: Black 0 at F1 removes White Root at F7.

W: White 3 at H4 removes Black 9 at H8.

B: Black Root at B8 moves to B7.

W: White 2 at A2 removes Black 7 at G2.

B: Black 3 at C3 moves to C1.

W: White 5 at A1 moves to A7 to remove Black 5 at I7 and Black Root at B7.

Game is over. All Black Roots removed and the White side wins the game.

7. New Math Chess Game 07 – 2A2S.

2 Additions + 2 Subtractions

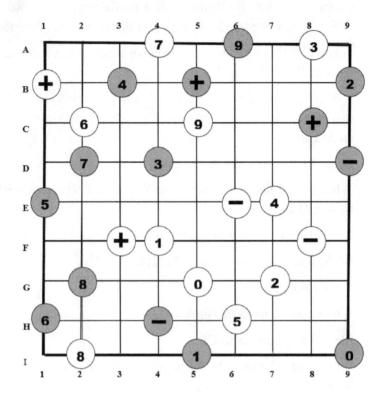

W: White 6 at C2 jumps over its partner White 9 at C5 to remove Black Addition at C8.

B: Black 4 at B3 removes White Addition at F3.

W: White 0 at G5 jumps over its partner White 9 at C5 to remove Black Addition at B5.

B: Black 6 at H1 jumps over its partner Black 5 at E1 to remove White Addition at B1.

W: White 2 at G7 moves to G9 to remove Black 2 at B9, Black 0 at I9 and Black Subtraction at D9.

("Black 2 (Black -) *White 2*, Black 0" is a Partial Equality of Subtraction).

B: Black Subtraction at H4 removes White 1 at F4.

W: White 4 at E7 moves to F7 to remove Black 4 at F3 and Black Subtraction at F4.

("***White 4*** (Black -) Black 4" is a Partial Equality of Subtraction).

Game is over. All Black Operators removed and the White side wins the game.

8. New Math Chess Game 08 – 2M2D.

2 Multiplications + 2 Divisions

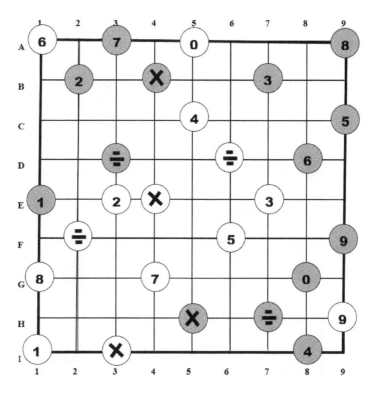

W: White 4 at C5 moves to B5 to remove Black 2 at B2, Black 3 at B7 and Black Multiplication at B4.

("Black 2 (Black x) ***White 4,*** Black 3" is a Partial Equality of Multiplication).

B:	Black 7 at A3 moves to A4 to remove White 7 at G4 and White Multiplication at E4.
	(*"**Black 7** (White x) White 7"* is a Partial Equality of Multiplication).
W:	White 3 at E7 removes Black Division at H7.
B:	Black Multiplication at H5 removes White 4 at B5.
W:	White 0 at A5 removes Black Multiplications at B5.
B:	Black 4 at I8 moves to H8.
W:	White 2 at E3 removes Black 1 at E1.
B:	Black Division at D3 removes White Multiplication at I3.
W:	White 1 at I1 removes Black Division at I3.

Game is over. All Black Operators removed and the White side wins the game.

9. New Math Chess Game 09 – 2P2R.

2 Powers + 2 Roots

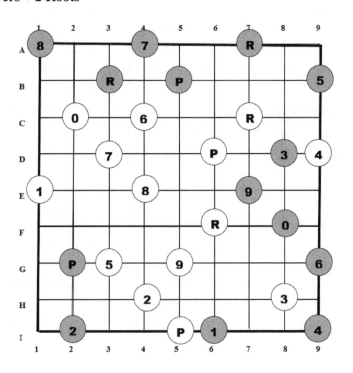

W: White 5 at G3 jumps over its partner White 7 at D3 to remove Black Root at B3.

At the new position, white 5 removes Black 5 at B9 and Black Power at B5.

("*White 5* (Black P) Black 5" is a Partial Equality of Power).

B: Black 4 at I9 jumps over its partner Black 1 at I6 to remove White Power at I5.

W: White 4 at D9 moves to A9 to remove Black 8 at A1 and Black Root at A7.

("*White 4* (Black R) Black 8" is a Partial Equality of Root as $\sqrt{4} = 2$ and $\sqrt[3]{8} = 2$ are two equal Partial Values of the Root).

B: Black 9 at E7 removes White Root at C7.

W: White 1 at E1 moves to G1 to remove Black Power at G2.

("*White 1* (Black P) Black 9" is a Partial Equality of Power as $1^2 = 1$ and $9^2 = 81$ are two equal Partial Values of the Root)

Game is over. All Black Operators removed and the White side wins the game.

10. New Math Chess Game 10 – 1A1S1M1D.

1 Addition + 1 Subtraction + Multiplication + 1 Division

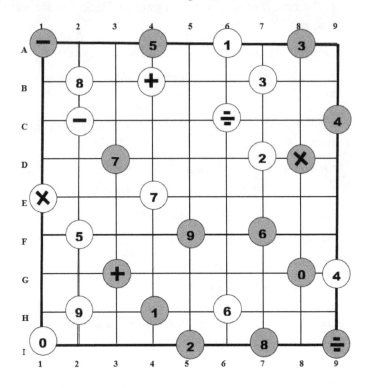

W: White Multiplication at E1 removes Black Subtraction at A1.

B: Black 7 at D3 moves to D2 to remove White 9 at H2, White 5 at F2, White 8 at B2 and White Subtraction at C2.

("***Black 7***, White 9 (White -) White 8"   as (10+7) – 9 = 8

"***Black 7***, White 5 (White -) White 8"   as (10+5) – 7 = 8

are two Partial Equalities of Subtraction).

W: White 4 at G9 moves to D9 to remove Black 7 at D2 and Black Multiplication at D8.

("***White 4*** (Black x) Black 7, White 2" is a Partial Equality of Multiplication).

B: Black 4 at C9 removes White Division at C6.

W: White 4 at D9 removes Black Division at I9.

B: Black 4 at C6 moves to C4 to remove White Addition at B4.

("Black 5 (White +) **Black 4**, Black 1" is a Partial Equality of Addition).

W: White 0 at I1 moves to G1 to remove Black 0 at G8 and Black Addition at G3.

Game is over. All Black Operators removed and the White side wins the game.

11. New Math Chess Game 11 – 1A1S1M1D.

1 Addition + 1 Subtraction + Multiplication + 1 Division

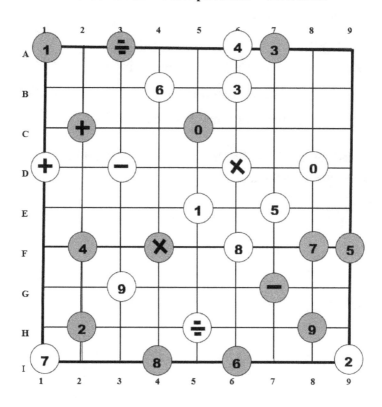

W: White 9 at G3 removes Black Subtraction at G7.

B: Black Division at A3 removes White Subtraction at D3.

W: White Addition at D1 removes Black Division at D3.

B: Black 9 at H8 moves to H6 to remove White 4 at A6, White 3 at B6, White 8 at F6 and White Multiplication at D6.

("***Black 9***, White 8 (White x) White 4, White 3" is a Partial Equality of Multiplication as 9 x 8 = 72 and 3 x 4 = 12 are two equal Partial Values of the Multiplication).

W: White 6 at B4 moves to B2 to remove Black 2 at H2, Black 4 at F2 and Black Addition at C2.

("***White 6*** (Black +) Black 2, Black 4" is a Partial Equality of Addition).

B: Black 3 at A7 moves to A3.

W: White Addition at D3 removes Black 3 at A3.

B: Black 1 at A1 removes White Addition at A3.

W: White Division at H5 removes Black 9 at H6.

B: Black 6 at I6 removes White Division at H6.

Game is over. All White Operators removed and the Black side wins the game.

12. New Math Chess Game 12 – 1A1S1M1D.

1 Addition + 1 Subtraction + Multiplication + 1 Division

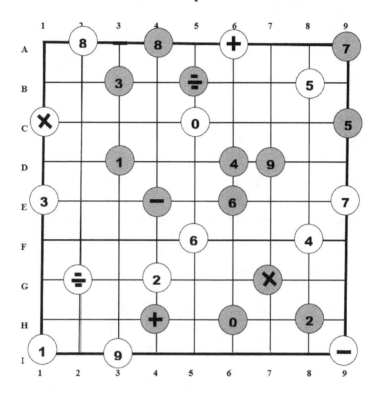

W: White 0 at C5 moves to C4 to remove Black 8 at A4 and Black Subtraction at E4.

(*"**White 0**, Black 8 (Black -) White 2"* is a Partial Equality of Subtraction as (0 + 10) – 8 = 2 and 2 are two equal Partial Values of the Subtraction).

B: Black 3 at B3 moves to B1 to remove White 3 at E1, White 1 at I1 and White Multiplication at C1.

(*"**Black 3** (White x) White 3, White 1"* is a Partial Equality of Multiplication).

W: White 9 at I3 moves to I7 to remove Black 9 at D7 and Black Multiplication at G7.

B: Black 6 at E6 jumps over its partner Black 4 at D6 to remove White Addition at A6.

W: White 0 at C4 jumps over its partner White 2 at G4 to remove Black Addition at H4.

B: Black Division at B5 removes White 6 at F5.

W: White 4 at F8 removes Black Division at F5.

Game is over. All Black Operators removed and the White side wins the game

13. New Math Chess Game 13 – 1A1S1M1D.

1 Addition + 1 Subtraction + Multiplication + 1 Division

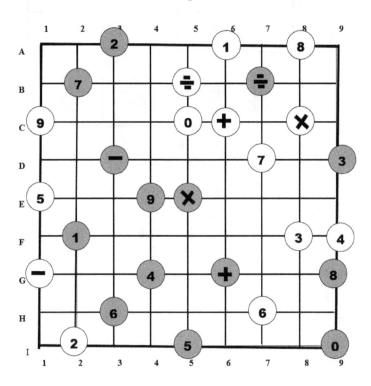

W: White 6 at H7 moves to G7 to remove Black 8 at G9, Black 4 at G4 and Black Addition at G6.

("**White 6**, Black 8 (Black +) Black 4" is a Partial Equality of Addition).

B: Black 6 at H3 moves to H1 to remove White 9 at C1, White 5 at E1 and White Subtraction at G1.

("**Black 6** (White -) White 9, White 5" is a Partial Equality of Subtraction as 6 and (10+5) – 9 = 6 are two equal Partial Values of the Subtraction).

W: White 6 at G7 moves to G5 to remove Black 5 at I5 and Black Multiplication at E5.

("**White 6,** Black 5 (Black x) White 0" is a Partial Equality of Multiplication, as 6 x 5 = 30 and 0 are 2 equal Partial Values of Multiplication).

B: Black 6 at H1 moves to H8 to remove White 3 at F8, White 8 at A8 and White Multiplication we C8.

("**Black 6**, White 3 (White x) White 8" is a Partial Equality of Multiplication).

W: White 7 at D7 removes Black Division at B7.

At its new position, White 7 continues to remove Black 7 at H2.

("**White 7** (White ÷) Black 7" is a Partial Equality of Division).

B: Black 1 at F2 moves to F6 to remove White 1 at A6 and White Addition at C6.

("**Black 1** (White +) White 1" is Partial Equality of Addition).

W: White 2 at I2 moves to I3 and removes Black 2 at A3 and Black Subtraction at D3.

Game is over. All Black Operators removed and the White side wins the game

14. New Math Chess Game 14 – 1A1S1M1D1P1R.

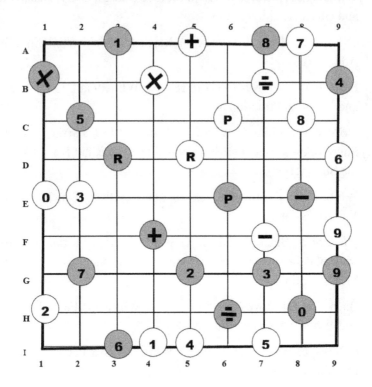

W: White Division at B7 jumps over its partner White Multiplication at B4 to remove Black Multiplication at B1.

B: Black Addition at F4 removes White Multiplication at B4.

W: White Division at B1 removes Black Addition at B4.

B: Black Division at H6 jumps over its partner Black Power at E6 to remove White Power at C6.

W: White 7 at A8 jumps over its partner White 8 at C8 to remove Black Subtraction at E8.

B: Black 4 at B9 removes White Division at B4.

W: White Root at D5 removes Black 2 at G5, then continues to remove Black 7 at G2 and Black 9 at G9.

("Black 7 (*White R*) Black 9" is a Partial Equality of Root, as $\sqrt[3]{20+7} = 3$, $\sqrt{9} = 3$ are two equal Partial Values of the Root).

B: Black 3 at G7 removes White Root at G5.

W: White 0 at E1 jumps over its partner White 3 at E2 to remove Black Power at E6.

B: Black Division at C6 removes White 0 at E6.

W: White 6 at D9 removes Black Root at D3.

B: Black 5 at C2 removes White 3 at E2.

W: White Subtraction at F7 moves to F6.

B: Black Division at E6 removes White Subtraction at F6.

W: White 9 at E9 removes Black Division at F6.

Game is over. All Black Operators removed and the White side wins the game.

15. New Math Chess Game 15 – 1A1S1M1D1P1R.

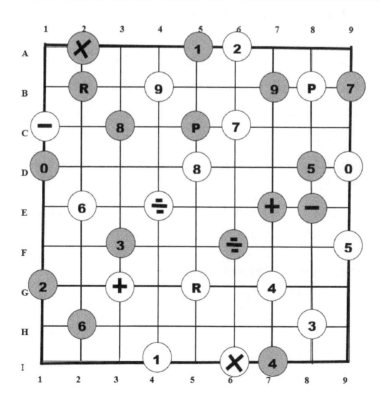

W: White Division at E4 removes Black Addition at E7.

B: Black Subtraction at E8 removes White Division at E7.

W: White 6 at E2 removes Black Subtraction sat E7.

B: Black 2 at G1 jumps over its partner Black 0 at D1 to remove White Subtraction at C1.

W: White Multiplication at I6 removes Black Division at F6.

B: Black 7 at B9 removes White 9 at B4 and White Power at B8.

("**Black 7** (White P) White 9" is a Partial Equality of Power, as 7^2 = 49 and 9^3 = 729 are 2 equal Partial Values of the Power).

W: White Addition at G3 removes Black 3 at F3.

B: Black 8 at C3 removes White Addition at F3.

W: White 3 at H8 removes Black 6 at H2.

B: Black 4 at I7 removes White 1 at I4.

W: White 4 at G7 jumps over its partner White 6 at E7 to remove Black 9 at B7.

B: Black Power at C5 removes White 7 at C6.

W: White Multiplication at F6 removes Black Power at C6.

B: Black 2 at C1 removes White Multiplication at C6.

W: White 5 at F9 removes Black 8 at F3.

B: Black 4 at I4 moves to I5 to remove White 8 at D5 and White Root at G3.

("**Black 4** (White R) White 8" is a Partial Equality of Root as $\sqrt{4}$ = 2 and $\sqrt[3]{8}$ = 2 are 2 equal Partial Values of the Root).

Game is over. All White Operators removed and the Black side wins the game.

16. New Math Chess Game 16 – 1A1S1M1D1P1R.

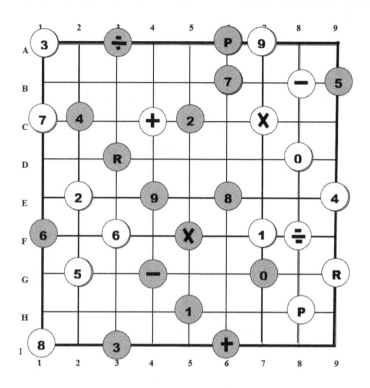

W: Blue 0 at D8 removes Black Root at D3.

B: Black 1 at H5 removes White Power at H8.

W: White 6 at F3 jumps over its partner White 0 at D3 to remove Black Division at A3.

B: Black Power at A6 removes White 6 at A3.

W: White 5 at G2 jumps over its partner White 2 at E2 to remove Black 4 at C2, then continues to remove Black 2 at C5.

("*White 5,* White 7 (White +) Black 2" is a Partial Equality of Addition).

B: Black 8 at E6 jumps over its partner Black 9 at E4 to remove White 2 at E2.

W: White 5 at C2 removes Black 8 at E2.

B: Black 9 at E4 moves to E7 to remove White 9 at A7, White 1 at F7 and White Multiplication at C7.

("***Black 9,*** White 1 (White x) White 9" is a Partial Equality of Multiplication).

W: White Division at F8 removes Black Multiplication at F5.

B: Black Subtraction at G4 removes White Addition at C4.

W: White 7 at C1 remove Black Subtraction at C4.

B: Black 6 at F1 removes White Division at F5.

W: White 3 at A1 removes Black Power at A3.

B: Black 1 at H8 removes White Subtraction at B8.

W: White Root at G9 removes Black 0 at G7.

B: Black 9 at E7 removes White Root at G7.

Game is over. All White Operators removed and the Black side wins the game.

17.   New Math Chess Game 17 – 1A1S1M1D1P1R.

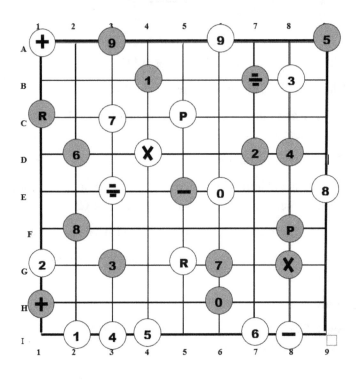

W: White Division at E3 removes Black Subtraction at E5.

B: Black 4 at D8 jumps over its partner Black 2 at D7 and removes White Multiplication at D4.

W: White 7 at C3 moves to B3 to remove Black 1 at B4 and Black Division at B7.

("***White 7***, Black 1 (Black ÷) White 3" is a Partial Equality as (20+1) ÷ 7 = 3 and 3 are two equal Partial Values of the Division).

B: Black Root at C1 removes White Addition at A1.

W: White Subtraction at I8 removes Black Multiplication at G8.

B: Black 2 at D7 moves to G7 to remove White 2 at G1 and White Root at G5.

("***Black 2*** (White R) White 2) is a Partial Equality of the Root).

W: White Subtraction at G8 removes Black Power at F8.

B: Black 8 at F2 removes White Subtraction at F8.

W: White Power at C5 moves to C3 to remove Black 9 at A3 and Black 3 at G3.

("Black 9 (***White P***) Black 3" is a Partial Equality of Power, as $9^3 = 729$ and $3^2 = 9$ are two equal Partial Values of the Power).

B: Black 7 at G6 moves to G3 to remove White 7 at B3 and White Power at C3.

("***Black 7*** (White P) White 7" is a Partial Equality of Power).

W: White 3 at B8 remove Black 8 at F8.

B: Black Addition at H1 moves to H5.

W: White Division at E5 removes Black Addition at H5.

B: Black 0 at H6 removes White Division at H5.

Game is over. All White Operators removed and the Black side wins the game.

18. New Math Chess Game 18 – 1A1S1M1D1P1R.

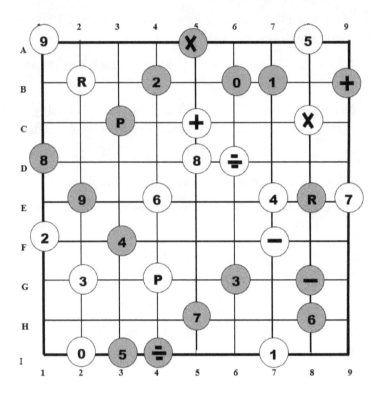

W: White 6 at E4 jumps over its partner White 4 at E7 to remove Black Root at E8.

At its new position, White 6 continues to remove Black 6 at H6 and Black Subtraction at G8.

("*White 6* (Black -) Black 6" is a Partial Equality of Subtraction).

B: Black Division at I4 removes White Power at G4, then continues to remove White 3 at G2.

("White 3 (*Black* ÷) Black 3" is a Partial Equality of Division).

W: White 7 at E9 removes Black Addition at B9.

B: Black Multiplication at A5 removes White Addition at C5.

W: White Root at B2 moves to D2 to remove Black 8 at D1.

("Black 8 (*White R*) White 8" is a Partial Equality of Root).

B:	Black Power at C3 jumps over its partner Black Multiplication at C5 to remove White Multiplication at C8.
W:	White 2 at F1 moves to H1.
B:	Black 4 at F3 removes White Subtraction at F7.
W:	White 2 at H1 moves to H4 and removes Black 2 at B4 and Black Division at G4.
B:	Black 5 at I3 moves to A3.
W:	White 2 at H4 removes Black 7 at H5.
B:	Black Multiplication at C5 moves to C2.
W:	White Root at D2 removes Black Multiplication at C2.
B:	Black Power at C8 removes White Root at C2.
W:	White 9 at A1 moves to A2 to remove Black 9 at E2 and Black Power at C2.

("*White 9* (Black P) Black 9" is a Partial Equality of Power)

Game is over. All Black Operators removed and the White side wins the game.

19. New Math Chess Game 19 – 1A1S1M1D1P1R.

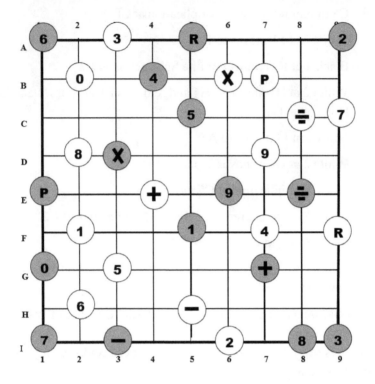

W: White 0 at B2 moves to B1 to remove Black 0 at G1 and Black Power at E1.

("*White 0* (Black P) Black 0" is a Partial Equality of Power).

B: Black 5 at C5 jumps over its partner Black 1 at F5 to remove White Subtraction at H5.

W: White 5 at G3 removes Black Addition at G7.

B: Black 7 at I1 moves to C1 to remove White 7 at C9 and White Division at C8.

("*Black 7* (White ÷) White 7" is a Partial Equality of Division).

W: White Addition at E4 removes Black 9 at E6.

B: Black Division at E8 removes White Addition ae E6.

W: White Multiplication at B6 removes Black Division at E6.

B: Black 2 at A9 moves to A7 to remove White 4 at F7 and White Power at B7.

("***Black 2*** (White P) While 4" is a Partial Equality of Power, as $2^2 = 4$ and $4^3 = 64$ are two equal Partial Values of the Power).

W: White 6 at H2 moves to I2 to remove Black 8 at I8 and Black Subtraction at I3.

("***White 6*** (Black -) Black 8, White 2" is a Partial Equality of Power)

B: Black 3 at I9 removes White Root at F9.

W: White 3 at A3 removes Black Multiplication at D3.

B: Black 2 at A7 moves to A6 to remove White 2 at I6 and White Multiplication at E6.

Game is over. All White Operators removed and the Black side wins the game.

20. New Math Chess Game 20 – 1A1S1M1D1P1R.

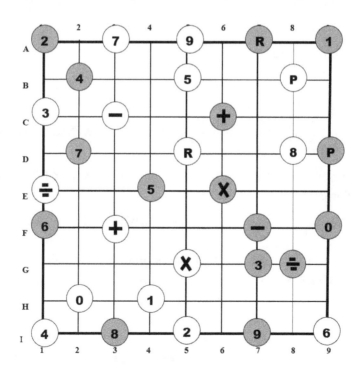

W: White Addition at F3 removes Black Subtraction at F7.

B: Black Root at A7 removes White Addition at F7.

W: White 9 at A5 moves to A7 to remove Black 3 at G7, Black 9 at I7 and Black Root at F7.

("*White 9* (Black R) Black 3" is a Partial Equality of Root as $\sqrt{40+9} = 7$ and $\sqrt[3]{340+3} = 7$ are two equal Partial Values of the Root).

("*White 9* (Black R) Black 9" is also a Partial Equality of the Root)

B: Black 8 at I3 moves to D3 to remove White 8 at D8 and White Root at D5.

("*Black 8* (White R) White 8" is a Partial Equality of the Root).

W: White Subtraction at C3 removes Black Addition at C6.

B: Black Multiplication at E6 removes White Subtraction at C6.

W: White 3 at C1 removes Black Multiplication at C6.

B: Black 5 at E4 removes White Division at E1.

W: White Multiplication at G5 removes Black Division at G8.

B: Black 0 at F9 moves to F8.

W: White 7 at A3 removes Black 8 at D3.

B: Black 5 at E1 moves to E8.

W: White Power at B8 moves to B6.

B: Black 5 at E8 jumps over its partner Black 0 at F8 to remove White Multiplication at G8.

W: White 1 at H4 moves to H9 to remove Black 1 at B9 and Black Power at D9.

("*White 1* (Black P) Black 1" is a Partial Equality of Power)

Game is over. All Black Operators removed and the White side wins the game.

LIST OF DEFINITIONS, CONVENTIONS, RULES

List of Definitions

Definition 1: A Digit attaches to an Operator if it is on the same line (horizontal or vertical) with the Operator and no other Operator exists between them. (Page 7)

Definition 2: The sums 15, 10, 11, 9 are the *left Partial Sums* or the *left Partial Values* of the operator Addition. (Page 9)

Definition 3: The sum 10 is the *right Partial Sum* or the *right Partial Value* of the operator Addition. (Page 9)

Definition 4: The differences 2, 8, 1, 9 are the *left Partial Differences* or the *left Partial Values* of the operator Subtraction. (Page 9)

Definition 5: The differences 4, 6 are the *right Partial Differences* or the *right Partial Values* of the operator Subtraction. (Page 10)

Definition 6: The products 120, 24, 30, 20 are the *left Partial Products* or the *left Partial Values* of the operator Multiplication. (Page 10)

Definition 7: Product 21 is the *right Partial Product* or the *right Partial Value* of the operator Multiplication. (Page 10)

Definition 8: The quotients 4 and 9 are the *left Partial Quotients* or the *left Partial Values* of the operator Division. (Page 11)

Definition 9: The quotient 9 is the *right Partial Quotient* or the *right Partial Value* of the operator Division. (Page 11)

Definition 10: The Powers 36, 216, 16, 64, 25, 125 are the *left Partial Powers* or the *left Partial Values* of the operator Power. (Page 12)

Definition 11: The Powers 49, 343, 9, 27 are the *right Partial Powers* or the *right Partial Values* of the operator Power. (Page 12)

Definition 12: The square/cube roots 4, 6, 2, 8, 5 are the *left Partial Roots* or the *left Partial Values* of the operator Root. (Page 13)

Definition 13: The cube roots 3 and 7 are the *right Partial Roots* or the *right Partial Values* of the operator Root. (Page 13)

Definition 14: Two Partial Values on the same line but different sides of an Operator are *Partially Equal* if they have the *same last Digit*. (Page 15)

Definition 15: The Digits of two equal Partial Values of an Operator and the Operator form a *Partial Equality* of this Operator. (Page 15)

Definition 16: Two Operator pieces of the same player form an *Operator Pair* when they are on the same line (horizontal or vertical) and not separated by any Digit or Operator piece of any player. (Page 19)

Definition 17: Two Digit pieces of the same player form a *Digit Pair* when they are on the same line (horizontal or vertical) and not separated by any Digit or Operator piece of any player. (Page 20)

List of Conventions

Convention 1: *Subtraction deals with only two terms. If the first term is less than the second one, increase it by 10.* (Page 9)

Convention 2: *Division deals with only two terms. If a dividend is not divisible by the divisor, increase it by a multiple of 10 so that a one-digit quotient can be obtained.* (Page 10)

Convention 3: *A multiple of 10 is added to a Digit so that a one-digit square Root or cube Root can be obtained.* (Page 12)

Convention 4: *A single Digit attached to a multi-term Operator is a Partial Value of this Operator.* (Page 13)

List of Rules

R01 – One Move in turn……..………………….……………………….. 21

R02 – Removal by Operator piece …………………………………… 21

R03 – Removal by two single Digit pieces on a line ………………. 22

R04 – Removal by single Digit and Operator pieces on a line …….. 22

R05 – Removal by Operator Pair …………………………………… 23

R06 – Removal by Digit Pair ……………………………………… 24

R07 – Removal by Partial Equality of Operator …………………... 25

R08 – Multiple Removals by Operator pieces ……………………… 32

R09 – Extended Effect of Operator pieces ……………...…………… 35

R10 – Multiple Removals by Digit pieces ……………......…………… 39

R11 – Extended Effect of Digit pieces ……………………………... 39

R12 – Removals without moving …………………………………… 42

ABOUT THE AUTHOR

Dr George Ho (aka Ho V Hoa) graduated from the University of Pedagogy, section Mathematics, in Vietnam (1962). He holds a Bachelor of mathematics (1965) and a Doctorate ès Sciences (March 1975) at the University of Sciences in Saigon, Vietnam. He spent 7 years in high school, teaching mathematics for Year 12 students (1962-1969), and 10 years in the Department of Theoretical Physics of University of Sciences in Saigon, Vietnam. He came to Australia in 1980 and finished the Graduate Diploma in Data Processing with Distinction at the NSW Institute of Technology, Sydney, in 1982. He last position was a project leader at the Credit Reference Association of Australia (CRAA). He retired in 2006.

www.ingramcontent.com/pod-product-compliance
Lightning Source LLC
LaVergne TN
LVHW041630170825
818877LV00006B/362